The Top *10* Highly Profitable, Proven, Time-Tested Secrets to Create the Ultimate First and Last Impression with Your Client

By John Di Lemme

The Top *10* Highly Profitable, Proven,
Time-Tested Secrets to Create the Ultimate First
and Last Impression with Your Client
Copyright © 2014 by John Di Lemme

Di Lemme Development Group, Inc.
931 Village Boulevard, Suite 905-366
West Palm Beach, Florida 33409-1939
(561) 847-3467
www.LifestyleFreedomClub.com

All rights reserved. No part of this book may be used or reproduced by any means, graphics, electronic, or mechanical, including photocopying, recording, taping or by any information storage retrieval system without the written permission of the author. Please contact Team@LifestyleFreedomClub.com to request permission to use quotes from this material.

This book is designed to provide competent and reliable information regarding the subject matters covered. However, it is sold with the understanding that the author is not engaged in rendering legal, financial, or other professional advice. Laws and practices often vary from state to state and if legal or other expert assistance is required, the services of a professional should be sought. The author specifically disclaims any liability that is incurred from the use and/or application of the contents of this book.

ISBN: 978-1-304-74760-0

About the Author

In September 2001, John Di Lemme founded Di Lemme Development Group, Inc., a company known worldwide for its role in expanding the personal-development industry. As President and CEO, John strives for excellence in every area of his business and believes that you must surround yourself with a like-minded team in order to stay on top of your game.

In addition to building a successful company, John has changed lives around the globe as an international motivational speaker who has spoken at over 500 venues. Over the past thirteen years, he has shared the stage with the best of the best, including Rich Devos, Denis Waitley, Jim Rohn, and Les Brown only to name a few. John has also been interviewed countless times and featured on many programs. This is truly an amazing feat for someone who was clinically diagnosed as a stutterer at a very young age and told that he would never speak fluently.

John truly believes that everyone needs personal development to reach their full potential in life, and his determination to reach all forms of media with his motivational messages has catapulted his career. John has produced over 450 products and is an accomplished author of thirteen books, including his best-selling book, "7 Principles to Live a Champion Life." As a strategic business coach and small business expert, John teaches his students who include doctors, lawyers, entrepreneurs, consultants, CEOs of million-dollar companies and various other occupations that are thriving in a so-called poor economy. John's success with his students has made him one of the most highly sought-after business coaches in the world.

John's passion is to teach others how to live a champion life despite the label that society has placed on them. Through his books, CDs, DVDs, live seminars, intensive boot camps, tele-classes, strategic business coaching, Closing & Marketing University, Millionaire Affirmation Academy, Why Warrior University, and Lifestyle Freedom Club memberships, John has made success a reality for thousands worldwide.

Introduction

Entrepreneurs are very different people. They have a different mindset. They live and breathe for their businesses.

In fact, true entrepreneurs weave business into every part of their lives. These dedicated people don't separate business from pleasure. For them, business *is* a pleasure. That's why entrepreneurs are emotionally stable. Part of that emotional stability comes from leading a well-structured life.

A successful business must have a solid structure, and that structure must be based on great long-term relationships with clients. To build those relationships, entrepreneurs must provide problem-solving products and services in truly impressive ways. After all, people often say:

2 Impression

"You only get one chance to make a great first impression."

That's true. But I also believe in creating an extraordinary first *and* last impression. Together, both elements create a *lasting* impression. In other words, people remember you. Their memory of you and your business *lasts* instead of fading away.

People who remember you and your business will automatically recommend you to friends and family.

Those recommendations are known as referrals, and you shouldn't have to ask for referrals. When you focus on solving your clients' problems and show that you care about people, you'll get referrals *automatically and consistently forever*.

And when you show honesty, integrity, and dedication in your business, those character traits will carry over into your personal life, forming the core of your personality. Then people will want to be around you. They'll admire you and trust you. That's why you shouldn't turn your business on and off like a light switch by consciously separating your business life from your personal life.

After all, you can't be two people. So, why should you lead *two* lives?

To lead one life and experience the happiness of success, you must make a commitment to producing extraordinary value for your clients.

When you're emotionally sound enough to make that commitment, you'll be willing to invest in your clients by providing an impressive level of service. And your clients will give you a return on your investment by committing to a long-term business relationship with you. They'll be impressed by you and the tremendous value of what you offer, and they'll buy products and services from you again and again as a result.

So, make a great impression on people by following *The Top *10* Highly Profitable, Proven, Time-Tested Secrets to Create the Ultimate First and Last Impression with Your Client*. These secrets are derived from the ten letters that comprise the word, IMPRESSION.

Each letter is associated with different parts of the goal that you'd like to achieve in business. That goal is your Why, your reason for striving for success.

Put yourself on the path to success by learning what the following ten letters stand for in the word, impression:

1. **I** stands for introduce and initiate.
2. **M** stands for memory and mindset.
3. **P** stands for priority, participation, and presence.
4. **R** stands for relationships, revival, restoration, and responses.
5. **E** stands for experience, engage, and experiment.
6. **S** stands for surprise bonuses.
7. **S** also stands for shocking, solution, secret, shortcut, spoken for, and sold out.
8. **I** stands for involvement.
9. **O** stands for over-delivering.
10. **N** stands for non-negotiable.

Absolutely FREE Marketing Book for You!
57 Must Use Marketing Words
www.FreeMarketingWords.com

Secret #1

I: Introduce and Initiate

When someone is **introduced** to you and your business, what is that person's first impression? The answer to that question is important. The answer will help you to be true to yourself. As a result, you'll see how well you present yourself.

Contrary to popular belief, people *do* judge a book by its cover. The cover gives them an initial impression of the quality of the text. If the cover contains an unappealing photo or illustration, people won't buy the book.

Your appearance is similar to a book cover. People will judge you by observing your physical appearance or by listening to the sound of your voice. If you look bad or sound unfriendly, no one will want to buy what you're marketing.

And remember that, in business, you're not just selling a product or service. You're selling yourself. That fact makes it vital for you to present yourself and your office professionally.

Prepare to introduce yourself by making sure you're dressed for success. Wear high-quality clothes that make you look better than your competitors. Your hair should look good, too. Get it cut and styled.

Next, keep your breath fresh. Stock your office with breath mints or mouthwash. There's nothing worse than rancid-smelling breath. If you have to *wonder* if your breath smells bad, you're already in trouble.

If you operate a business with employees, team members, or even subcontractors have them wear uniforms. Don't make a potential client *wonder* who works for your company.

It's also important not to assume that a client knows your name and business title. Wear a name tag that lists both. Your client will take comfort in having basic information about you.

You should also ensure that your office is clean and comfortable. Keep the temperature at the right level. The rooms shouldn't be too hot or too cold. When it comes to clients, there should be no penny-pinching.

There should also be some music playing in your office. Music relaxes people and puts them in a relaxed mood.

And when it's time to **initiate** a conversation with a client, make eye contact and pay attention to what the person says. Don't answer calls on your cell phone or send text messages while talking to your client. Pay attention!

Actively listen to your client. By listening, you'll remember things that can help you establish a long-term relationship with that person. In other words, your memory will help you build your business.

Secret #2

M: Memory and Mindset

Having an excellent **memory** is an important part of succeeding in business. For example, you can use your memory to impress a client. How? Show that you remember something that's important to your clients such as their birthday, anniversary, or wedding.

Follow up by sending them a card or free bonus product that shows that you remembered a special occasion in their life. Your gesture of kindness will impress them, and the bonus product will surprise them. That's why I often refer to these bonus products as *surprise* bonuses.

Remembering things that are important to your client should become a habit. A habit is automatic. It sets your mind on automatic pilot. For that reason, a habit can be thought of as a **mindset**.

The professionals who run the Ritz-Carlton Hotel have a certain mindset. They feel that their hotel guests should be treated to a luxurious experience. That experience is embodied by the finest service.

Amazing service starts right after you enter a Ritz-Carlton Hotel.

When you check in, the front-desk clerk will walk out from behind the counter, greet you, and give you your room key.

The clerk is following predetermined standards of service. In fact, the Ritz-Carlton's Website lists those standards as "a warm and sincere greeting..., anticipation and fulfillment of each guest's needs, [and a] fond farewell."

The employees at the hotel anticipate that guests will want a hassle-free check-in process. After all, if you're on a business trip, traveling may *already* have been a hassle.

Very often, when you arrive at a hotel, all you'll want is to get to your room, relax, unpack, and enjoy the resort.

The Ritz-Carlton has worked very hard to ensure that guests experience an efficient check-in process and are shown to their luxurious rooms without an extensive wait. According to the hotel's Website, the front-desk project team at the Ritz-Carlton in Osaka, Japan, reduced the check-in time by fifty percent. The staff fine-tuned the check-in process to give their guests an extraordinary first impression of the hotel. Fine-tuning this process is a consistent part of the staff's mindset.

You must develop the same mindset. You must fine-tune your business processes to satisfy your clients. That should be your priority.

Secret #3

P: Priority, Participation, and Presence

One of your major **priorities** in business should be to give top-notch customer service. From the beginning to the end of your meeting with a client, give them an experience that they will remember.

One of the best ways to create that experience is to anticipate your client's needs. If it's hot outside, have cold and room temperature bottles of water available. If it's raining outside, offer an umbrella. That way, they can walk to their car without getting wet. And don't ask your client to return the umbrella later. It's a special bonus that your client gets to keep. These extraordinary experiences will make an unbelievable impression on your clients, and they'll become your biggest fans.

Why do entrepreneurs need fans? Because fans give referrals, and referrals guarantee a business's growth.

Clients will become your fans when you actively participate in their lives. That active **participation** stems from your anticipating and acting on their needs.

A client shouldn't have to *ask* you for something. You should automatically *provide* it. Doing so is part of the mindset of successful entrepreneurs.

Smart entrepreneurs make a great impression when doing business. Their ability to anticipate a person's needs gives them a powerful **presence**.

People feel that way about *me*. They tell me: "John, when I'm around you, there's just something different about you. I just feel a presence."

There's a reason why people make that comment: I anticipate their needs and give them what they want *before* they know they want it. You can build a long-term relationship with someone by anticipating that person's needs.

Secret #4

R: Relationships, Revival, Restoration, and Responses

Business is all about **relationships**. One great way to build those relationships is to pick up the phone and call your clients. Talk to them. Ask them how they're doing and tell them how you can assist them in solving a problem that they're currently experiencing in business.

Letters are great, too. People like getting letters that are written to them personally. I'm not talking about form letters. I'm talking about letters that show you care. Those letters should mention specific things that you remember about your client.

In this day and age of e-mail and social networks, letter writing is practically a lost art. But you should **revive** the art of letter writing and use personal letters to build and deepen your business relationships.

When was the last time you received a heartfelt letter that was personally signed by someone? It's probably been a long time. But, when you opened the envelope and read the message, didn't the letter **restore** your faith and enhance your belief in that person or business?

When someone takes the time to send me a handwritten letter, it restores my faith in humanity. If the letter is from a business, it restores my faith in business. That's important because we live in an era when frauds and scams are ruining people's lives.

Nowadays, there's an abundance of unethical businessmen. Bernie Madoff is a prime example. He ran a hedge fund that turned out to be a giant Ponzi scheme. He fleeced investors of their hard-earned money.

Due to people like Madoff, you must put in extra effort to show that you have integrity. You must restore the faith of potential clients by building business relationships on a consistent, daily basis.

The act of restoring faith can also be physical. For example, you can update your office to change the experience your customers have when they arrive. Paint the walls if the paint is fading or chipping. Replace broken-down, dirty furniture. Make your place of business look fresh and inviting. That will make a great impression on people.

When my wife, Christie, and I invested in real estate in North Carolina and Florida, we invested money in restoration. We knew that in order to rent the properties to tenants, everything had to be clean, organized, and inviting. So, we installed upgrades such as high-end carpeting, ceiling fans, drapes, and other things that make a house into a home. We also repainted the walls with high-quality paint so that scuff marks could easily be removed.

As a result of our diligent restoration efforts, we've been able to successfully rent our properties. People love the interiors. Everything looks brand new. So, people have responded by renting from us. You can get the same positive **response** from clients by reviving the time-tested aspects of customer service.

Absolutely FREE Marketing Book for You!
57 Must Use Marketing Words
www.FreeMarketingWords.com

Impression

My grandfather, Papa D, taught me the most important principles of customer service.

He ran the family art gallery business, and he told me: "You never ever let a woman, a mother, a wife carry a piece of art out of the gallery. You have her pull her car up in front, and you open the car door and you put the art in the car."

Now, that's extreme customer service!

Secret #5

E: Experience, Engage, and Experiment

My grandfather's type of customer service is an **experience**, the very experience that leaves a great last impression. The *last* impression is the very *last* thing a client remembers about you before departing from your place of business.

One of the keys to leaving a great last impression is to **engage** in a heartfelt conversation with your client. And one way to start that conversation is to wear a name tag that displays the name of your home town.

My home town is Yonkers, New York. So, when a client from New York meets me and sees that state listed on my name tag, he will respond positively. He'll usually talk to me about all the great people and places from New York.

And we have such an awesome time talking to each other that I thank him profusely.

I say, "Thank you for coming to the Closing and Marketing University Boot Camp. Thank you for traveling from New York to see me. Have a safe trip home. I can't wait to see you again soon."

You see, when you develop great rapport with a client, you've successfully started the process of building a solid long-term business relationship. That type of relationship is the foundation of multi-billion dollar businesses like the Ritz-Carlton.

But you should **experiment** with different techniques for developing rapport. Find different things that you have in common with your clients. You'll learn that when you use those commonalities as conversation starters, you'll appreciate your clients. You'll be grateful to be around such interesting people.

Find different ways to appreciate the fact that your clients enrich your life.

Tell yourself, "My clients are assisting me to live the life I want. They're empowering me to live a lifestyle of freedom."

I love my millionaire champion students. They've given me the perfect lifestyle. That's one of the reasons why my business club is called the Lifestyle Freedom Club.

And I work very hard to show my appreciation to my students for the life they've helped me lead. I show my appreciation by giving them surprise bonuses as part of my company's extreme customer service.

Secret #6

S: Surprise Bonuses

Few things are more exciting than getting free bonus products, or **surprise bonuses**. People who receive them feel special.

I give away surprise bonuses regularly. After videotaping each monthly Lifestyle Freedom Club teaching, I send copies of the DVD to my students and I include a CD containing an audio recording of the DVD. The CD is an absolutely free surprise bonus.

It costs me more money to include the CD, but I don't care about the cost. I am consistently focused on my millionaire champion students.

And you should care about your clients. When you're good to them and show that you value them, they'll do business with you for a lifetime. That's the true meaning of the phrase, "lifetime value."

Build your business to develop lifetime value, not for a quick buck. Don't try to find a get-rich-quick scheme, and always remember that there's nothing fast about building a sustainable business.

Secret #7

S: Shocking, Solution, Secret, Shortcut, Spoken for, and Sold Out

You can build a sustainable business by giving away surprise bonuses. Your clients will feel they're getting the biggest bang for their buck.

My clients are always **shocked** when they receive surprise bonuses with an item that they ordered.

Recently, a client from Hawaii ordered a one-dollar CD from me. When she opens the package that my team sent, five CDs will fall out. Four of those CDs are surprise bonuses.

Those bonuses are my **solution** *and* my **secret** for thriving in a bad economy. They

Absolutely FREE Marketing Book for You!
57 Must Use Marketing Words
www.FreeMarketingWords.com

make first-time customers into lifetime customers, and lifetime customers are a bulletproof vest for a business in a so-called bad economy.

Remember that your clients *can* do business with someone else. There *are* other businesses that offer the same products and services that you offer. The only way to differentiate yourself from your competitors is to add extraordinary value for clients through top-notch, extreme customer service and surprise bonuses.

My recent customer from Hawaii *can* and *probably has* purchased motivational CDs and marketing CDs from other businesses. But *I* gave her bonuses. I showed her that I valued her. So, from now on, I doubt she'll go to anyone else but me for motivational products and marketing products.

She'll also find that my products can assist her in discovering the secrets to running a successful business. Many of those secrets can be found in my book, "57 Must-Use Words in Every Piece of Marketing You Do for Your Business."

In that book, I reveal to the world that there are powerful, proven, time-tested words that you can use to close sales on a consistent basis. Here are four of those words: **shortcut**, **secret**, **spoken for**, and **sold out**.

The next time you do a direct mail campaign for one of your products, use those four words.

In your sales letter, tell each client: "I wanted to reach out to you today because I know you're looking for a shortcut to success. We found the secret. And before all these products are spoken for and they're sold out, I want to make sure you get a chance to own yours now."

Secret #8

I: Involvement

Doing direct mail campaigns once in a while is great. But you must do far more to build long-term business relationships.

You must stay **involved** with your clients by communicating with them on a regular, consistent basis.

A key factor is to reward them for their business by sending them exclusive discount offers for past customers only.

And always remember to send birthday cards and holiday cards to your clients. Nothing impresses people more than being remembered on special occasions.

Another simple yet extraordinary idea is to include a handwritten note in each greeting card that you send out for your business. Mention something that's specific to your clients. That way, they will truly feel valued by you.

Secret #9

O: Over-Delivering

When you go out of your way to show that you value a client, you're **over-delivering**. And over-delivering is a key part of achieving success in business.

I routinely over-deliver for my students, as I actively listen to what they want at my events. For example, they like when I invite guest speakers but want *me* to personally conduct more teaching sessions at events.

That's why I'm going to speak on all three days of an upcoming Why Warrior Weekend event.

On the first day, I'll teach the ten life lessons that are detailed in my book, "10 Life Lessons on How to Find Your Why

NOW & Achieve Ultimate Success." On the second day, I'll talk about affirmations and how to speak with power. And, on the third day, I'll talk about closing and marketing.

I'm going to speak on all three days because I want to satisfy my students. My students are my customers, and I believe in extreme customer satisfaction. That's why I always try to over-deliver. You should over-deliver, too!

Secret #10

N: Non-negotiable

When you give a client a surprise bonus, you're over-delivering and practically guaranteeing customer satisfaction.

A satisfied customer is essential. Don't hold a debate with yourself about whether you should reward a customer. Make the reward **non-negotiable**.

When it comes to clients, you can't afford to be cheap. You can't afford *not* to give them surprise bonuses. The only way to earn more profits is to invest in your clients. Reward them for doing business with you.

After all, your clients *can* do business elsewhere. That's why it's essential that you make a commitment to producing more value than your competitors.

Tell yourself, "I'm committed to giving my clients extraordinary customer service and surprise bonuses. My commitment is non-negotiable, and that's a fact."

Your commitment will impress your clients and lead to supernatural, miraculous success.

Conclusion

Building a successful business *can* be easier than you ever thought possible. Simply adhere to The Top *10* Highly Profitable, Proven, Time-Tested Secrets to Create the Ultimate First and Last Impression with Your Clients.

Each letter in the word, IMPRESSION, will assist you in making a great impression on your clients. As a result, they'll remember you and become your biggest fans.

And fans are even better for your business than ads. Fans give referrals, and referrals guarantee a business' growth. With a constant stream of referrals, you'll be able to prosper in any economy.

Absolutely FREE Marketing Book for You!
57 Must Use Marketing Words
www.FreeMarketingWords.com

So, get started now. Build wealth by making a great first and last impression on your clients!

Let me know what you like best about this book and how you have chosen to implement the secrets for your business.

Send me an email at the following address: John@LifestyleFreedomClub.com. Feel free to give our team a call or text at (561) 847-3467 with any questions. You are a champion!

www.ingramcontent.com/pod-product-compliance
Lightning Source LLC
Chambersburg PA
CBHW072300170526
45158CB00003BA/1117